3 · 50

The Scope of Salvation:
Theatres of God's Drama

Lincoln Studies in Theology

Other titles in this series

The Word Preached to a Sister Church
by Adelbert Denaux
Lincoln Studies in Theology 1, 1996
ISBN 1–870561–11–2   £1.95

The Changing Face of God
by N. T. Wright, Keith Ward, and Brian Hebblethwaite
Lincoln Studies in Theology 2, 1996
ISBN 1–870561– 12–0   £2.95

Where Shall We Find God?
by Richard Burridge, Fraser Watts, and David Brown
Lincoln Studies in Theology 3, 1998
ISBN 1–870561– 15–1   £2.95

The Scope of Salvation:
Theatres of God's Drama

LINCOLN LECTURES IN
THEOLOGY 1998

Lincoln Cathedral Publications
1999

Published 1999 by Lincoln Cathedral Publications
Lincoln Cathedral, LN2 1PZ

ISBN   1 870561 17 1

Cover design by Max Marschner, Ampersand Designs, Lincoln LN5 8PN
Typeset and produced for the publisher by Yard Publishing Services, Sudbury CO10 2AG
Printed by Interprint Ltd, Malta

Cataloguing-in-Publication Data
  A catalogue entry for this publication is available from the British Library

Contents

Preface   7

    Vernon White,
    Chancellor of Lincoln

Salvation in Community   9

    Professor Mary Grey,
    University of Southampton

Salvation and the Self   23

    Professor David Ford,
    University of Cambridge

Salvation and Creation: 'All Things New'   40

    Professor Richard Bauckham and Professor Trevor Hart,
    University of St. Andrew's

Preface

SALVATION, as Mary Grey points out early on in these lectures, is not just a theological term. It has wider reference. But its wider use is often a debased currency. Could the *salvation* of a country or community ever really lie in interest rates? Hardly. Can the *salvation* of people ever lie in their own individual and self-positing selves? No – that's a lie of the Enlightenment. Could the *salvation* of the whole world ever evolve through human progress? Precious little sign of that.

The point lies in the rigour as well as the richness of the term. 'Salvation' will not simplify to money, human subjectivity, human science, or any sort of human effort. It may relate to all these things, but it will not reduce to them. It is inescapably theological as well. It only finds its full meaning in relation to God and, specifically, God in Christ. This much the three lectures clearly have in common.

They also reflect a common concern to balance immanence and transcendence. Each, in different ways, emphasizes that salvation is found in *relatedness*, rather than in isolation. It is found as a 'saving energy at work in community' (Mary Grey); it is experienced in worship as we 'face a God who faces all humanity and creation' (David Ford); it is proclaimed as God's purpose for us 'in our solidarity with the rest of ... creation' (Richard Bauckham and Trevor Hart). At the same time each lecture is concerned to resist the collapse of this relatedness into complete union. So we remain ourselves in relation to others, to creation, and to God, rather than becoming merged drops of water in a seamless sea of reality. And God remains a God who is 'other' and beyond, as well as immanent within community and nature. This is conveyed variously through the notion of 'boundaries' (Mary Grey), 'facing' (David Ford) and 'newness' (Richard Bauckham and Trevor Hart). It is a vital and distinctively Christian balance to strike.

In other respects the lectures differ in both substance and style. Substantially, the scope of each is divided much as the titles imply: salvation in community (including concerns for justice and ecology); personal (but not individualistic) salvation; the salvation of all things in history and nature. As for style, the reader will quickly pick up the varying pulse of the lectures. The texts convey much of the texture of the original addresses: the first notable for its passion, the second for its compressed elegance, and the last for its clarity. As with the previous titles in this series, I warmly commend this latest offering. It should engage anyone who is concerned to think more deeply about the possibilities of faith – and transformation – in a difficult world.

Vernon White, Chancellor of Lincoln

'Salvation in Community' was given on Tuesday, 10 March 1998.

'Salvation and the Self' was given on Tuesday, 17 March 1998.

'Salvation and Creation: "All Things New"' was given on Tuesday, 24 March 1998.

All these lectures were delivered in Edward King House, Lincoln.

Salvation in Community:
From Holy Well to Holy Waitrose

Mary Grey

L ET ME begin with a few images. The first three are taken from India, from the desert area of Rajasthan. From my involvement there over the past ten years, an all too frequent sight has been that of poor women, sometimes the Dalit or *untouchable* women, the outcasts, (beyond the caste system), walking ever further into the desert, iron pitchers or earthenware pots on their heads, sometimes two or three, in search of water. The wells have dried up and so the centre of community, the source of daily communal sharing has gone. 'With joy you shall draw water from the wells of salvation", said Isaiah (12.3) – but not here. When water vanishes (and here I will not go into the ecological and political reasons why the wells have dried up), community life dries up. Children die from drinking infected water; there is no agriculture and so the men drift to the city or migrate with the animals. In one area – the poorest in the district, called *Kala pani* or 'black water', because, in the days of the British, *Kala pani* was the place where criminals and undesirables were sent – there is a sense of desperation: this is the place where no teacher, no doctor will come – because the only water available tastes of salt. 'Where is salvation?' I ask – but also, *'where is community?'*

My second image is from Tamil Nadu in the south of India. Here among the communities of fisher-people, the women are considered to pollute the sea and are not allowed to enter it. (If you are a Latin Christian you may do so only on Christmas Day.) So, women do the work of mending the nets, sorting and gutting the fish, and doing all the marketing. This involves being away from home, travelling, enduring much sexual harassment and an incredible struggle to attain

9

a minimum wage. I use this as an example of the way the reality of experience differs according to whether you are man or woman; there is a gender difference in the experience of role division, of responsibilities and care for the household and children; and the question of who sustains communal life, and *how it is justly organised*, raises its head in an acute form.

But lest you think I am equating poverty and injustice with the *death* of community, let me cite the example of the slums of Bombay. Mile after mile of shelters line the side of the railway approaching down-town Bombay. There is no way that the rags, cardboard and sticks which form the roofs could possibly keep out the rain and cold. At one place the train crosses a river – both sides of which are lined by slums, the stench from which filled our railway carriage. Yet what is astounding is the courage and effort I saw to sustain dignity of living. The effort to wash clothes, to keep the children neatly dressed. Even the planting and caring for vegetable gardens on the railway line itself witnessed to this. Nothing should take away from the injustice of the level of poverty; nothing should allow us to idealise: yet there seems to me something to learn here both about community and about salvation.

My second set of images tries to capture what are the tangible glimpses of what we mean by *Christian* salvation today. The first group is known to you. The revivalist movements, the healing movements which span most of our denominations (and perhaps the most well-known is the Toronto Blessing), present a vibrant picture of people in community being healed in a dramatic way by publicly professing faith in Jesus Christ (granted the controversial nature of these: the question mark as to whether the so-called cures actually last; and the use of some of these movements to promote a conservative, right-wing view of Christianity – for example, the American Roman Catholic sister, Mother Angelica). Less dramatic, perhaps, are the charismatic prayer groups, the quieter healing services, the pilgrimages to Lourdes or places known for healing – all witnesses to healing in a community context through faith in Jesus

Christ. (There are secular counterparts too – in aromatherapy, meditation, nature cures.)

The third set of images are of what is most popularly thought of as salvation in Jesus Christ – the individualist model, perhaps summed up well by the song 'Amazing Grace'. The lines 'I was blind but now I see' offer a kind of paradigm for the dramatic conversion experience, with its scriptural origins in Paul's own Damascus road experience. And startling modern examples are seen in, for example, Malcolm X's conversion, or Nicky Cruse, the US gangster who became an evangelist. These do not properly belong to my theme of *community and salvation*, but it's important to note them, as often this is the most striking image of what salvation means in people's minds. And it points to what pastoral theology frequently finds incredibly difficult to deal with: the fact that many people think of salvation as a private affair, focusing on what God wants *me* to do to be saved. Yet, as my old Theology Professor said to me years ago: 'You may think you stand alone before God – but you have a very long tail: the rest of humanity stands behind you!'[1]

So, we have a diversity of images associated with salvation, many meanings of community, as well as a third strand interwoven, the figure of Jesus as Saviour and the way the understanding of this integrates the first two themes.

As we have seen, Jesus functions for many people solely and crucially as a personal and private saviour. *It was not always so.* Think of the mediaeval culture where the mystery plays which dramatised the unfolding of salvation filled the streets, their imagery and characters mirroring the familiar realities of peoples' lives – think of Mrs. Noah and her "gossips", to give one example. Echoes of these are left in some of the Christmas carols we still sing: 'On Christmas night all Christians sing ... news of our Saviour's birth' (Sussex Carol) is one example. Also, encapsulating the whole story in song:

[1]   Professor Johannes Van Bavel of the University of Louvain, Belgium, now retired, a distinguished Augustine scholar and an Augustinian priest.

> A virgin most pure, as the prophets do tell,
> Hath brought forth a baby. As it hath befell,
> To be our Redeemer, from death, Hell and sin,
> Which Adam's transgression hath wrapped us in
> ... And therefore be merry, set sorrows aside ...

There are echoes too, in art, music and sculpture – in the great Oratorios, in Christ Pantocrator of Byzantium, Christ in Majesty at Llandaff Cathedral: the mystery of salvation as part of the warp and woof of daily life.

But lest we succumb to nostalgia, let us also flag up the difficulties inherited with some of this traditional salvation doctrine. All too often, it removes the theatre of salvation to an other-worldly setting: 'God made us to serve him in this world and to be happy with him in the next', as my old Catechism taught me. Salvation could be seen as being saved from this world, this vale of tears, this mortal coil, these material and finite limits, where the spirit is frustrated from making transcendental leaps. Women, too, have difficulties with the traditional doctrine: salvation is portrayed as coming from a male saviour, a God imaged as male, and ministered through a priesthood and a sacramental system until recently exclusively male – and still so in my own Church. Finally, this doctrine was a very anthropocentric doctrine – human beings were alienated through sin and in need of saving: but the earth, the polluted soil, the damaged planet, was not seen as either subject or object in the theatre of redemption. (At least, not in mainstream doctrine: there has, however, been a deeper and almost forgotten strand inclusive of nature – which we are now beginning to recover. Tillich, for example, cried 'Nature, too, mourns for a lost good ....)[2]

But before I explore further the wrong turnings this doctrine has taken, I want to follow the clues which the linguistic trail offers: that is, what does the word salvation actually mean?

---

[2] Paul Tillich, 'Nature, too, mourns for a lost good' in *The Shaking of the Foundations*, (Fontana, *1954).*

EXCURSUS: THE LINGUISTIC TRAIL

First I want to avoid the trivialisation of the word in current use. In other words, its *metaphoric* use, as in *the salvation of the company/country lies in increasing interest rates;* or, savings seen as investment: the *'Jesus saves but not on my salary'* kind of joke.

Secondly, we need to recognise that *salvation* belongs to a cluster of words like liberation, redemption, atonement, freedom and reconciliation. They are all basically referring to God's action in Christ – but each of them is viewed from a particular dimension. The *special* focus of salvation is the issue here.

Salvation means both being saved in the sense of rescued, delivered, protected, preserved (from danger, from all kinds of evil, from death); it also means the state of being healed and whole, blessed, in good health as a result of this. Interestingly, there seem to be two roots of the word: in Latin, *salvus, salvare* – to save, be saved, translates the Greek *soteria*, deliverance, redemption – often referring to the action of the gods in classical Greek; and *salvus* from *olos*, whole; a 'salve, meaning an ointment which soothes and heals, even the soothing of wounded feelings.

There are numerous derivatives in Dutch, German, and French – *heiligwerden, heilworden* in Dutch (*holiness* and *wholeness* are very close). In German *seligkeit* means blessedness, salvation, but not in a privatised way – rather that a state of blessedness we call *shalom* (Arab *salaam)* which includes the well-being of the whole of creation, people, earth, trees and animals. The word integrity springs to mind. Is this a word that could link personal well-being with the communal, suggestive of the restoration of justice, and the discipline necessary for just conduct in public life?

A clue is given here, in these linguistic roots, that we need to recover an embodied theology of creation, the link between creation and redemption, before we can really understand the themes of community and salvation and an understanding of Christ in which they can be rooted.

Mary Grey

WRONG TURNINGS OF A DOCTRINE

This short linguistic glimpse poses new questions. If there is something about a *communal* state of blessedness inherent in the very concept of salvation, inclusive of the whole of creation, inclusive of bodily as well as spiritual realities, inclusive of all living things, sensitive to gender dimensions, with a sharp sense of justice, can we now identify and eliminate the wrong directions the doctrine has taken?

1. Let us agree that the prevalent individualism of our culture – seemingly ineradicable – has blinded us to the core meaning of salvation which reaches out to include, literally, the *commonwealth*, the well-being of entire communities. (This does not mean we should ignore the personal dimension – there is a journey we all must make alone – but the personal dimension is the theme of the next lecture in this series.) It might provide an important point of discussion to see how the Reformation Protestant insistence on the individual *coram Deo* somehow provided a ground for the focus on the individual – which would have disastrous consequences *philosophically* during the Enlightenment and *economically* with the rise of capitalism and the conquest of the so-called New World.

2. But even when we turn our attention away from the individual to that historical core of salvation doctrine which is the chosen *people* of God, whose trajectory of being chosen we follow through the Exodus experience, the Covenant on Sinai, and subsequent attempts to live out this covenant – a relationship which Christianity assumed when it began to image itself as the pilgrim people, wandering through the desert in search of the New Jerusalem (the predominant ecclesiological image of the Second Vatican Council) – *even this* trajectory of salvation history can be interpreted as elitist. Does God want to save *only* this group? What about all other world faiths and those outside them? What about earlier civilisations? What about the elitism which such a view of salvation history has encouraged?

Two examples will suffice. The Dutch Reformed Church in South Africa assumed the doctrine of *election as the chosen people* in such a way as to encourage and legitimate the doctrine of apartheid.

14

Secondly, an example from the Roman Catholic Church's tradition: the conviction of being the chosen people of the new covenant has led both to anti-Judaism as well as to the dangerous doctrine of *extra ecclesiam nulla salus* (no salvation outside the Church). The problem with this narrow interpretation of the salvation doctrine is that it has encouraged us to view Judaism as the mere backcloth to Christianity, superseded as soon as the new covenant of salvation arrived. Also, 'no salvation outside the Church' has encouraged Christians to assert the uniqueness and necessity of Christ in such a way as to underrate and undervalue the revelation of the sacred in world faiths. It also underpinned such historical atrocities as those committed by the crusades, the expulsion of the Jews from Spain, and the treatment of Islam.

3. Furthermore, the lack of a gender dimension to salvation has meant that social evils like domestic abuse and violence against women have co-existed with a doctrine of salvation which encouraged endurance, sacrifice and expiation in the name of holiness and 'being saved'.

4. Next, the lack of an ecological dimension has meant that vast areas of the earth have been exploited with express biblical sanction (using a text like that of Genesis, 'Have dominion over all living things'). The earth has been deemed expendable. The new heaven and the new Jerusalem are painted as being outside this planet in an extra-terrestrial location, as we are told, like the spoilt child with the toy, 'Never mind if you have broken your toy, Daddy will give you a new one'![3]

5. Finally, the understanding of Saviour required by this theology has become seen as an extra-terrestrial individual, 'coming down from heaven' in a kind of kenotic Christology, where 'he leaves all his glory behind', as the Christmas carol says. This kind of Saviour-figure – the contemporary version would be a kind of ET – is a Christian version

---

[3] I owe this insight to Catherine Keller: see 'Talk about the Weather: the Greening of Eschatology', in Carol Adams (ed.), *Ecofeminism and the Sacred* (New York, Continuum, 1993), pp. 30–49. Also, 'Eschatology, Ecology and a Green Ecumenacy', in *Ecotheology* 2, 1997, pp. 84–99.

of the *deus* or *dea ex machina* of the Greek tragedies, where, once the humans have got themselves into an impossible, inextricable fix, a divine figure (in an extraordinary trapeze affair – which must be the original ancestor of the Peter Pan flying episodes) flies in, a divine rescuer! But, heavens above (a paradoxical metaphor!) is it not the doctrine of *incarnation* we are talking about? And the incarnation is the *flesh-taking* of God. It is the ongoing embodiment of God in the full social and material realities of our universe.

What, then, does this mean for community and salvation? To start with, surely not being saved *from* the world and *from* community.

CHRIST – OUR COMMUNITY

Is there a way forward? Is there a way, in a contemporary world, which takes account of the fact that people are actually finding community not by and large in the churches but either via Internet or in the supermarkets? (For the latter, ironically, now resemble churches – hence my title 'From Holy Well to Holy Waitrose'. A journey through the aisles of Holy Waitrose or St Tesco's resembles a liturgical gathering: the word is proclaimed, the music of advertising permeates the air; the very architecture is dome or spire-shaped; the click of the till is the ritual of dismissal, or, as Ian Linden – General Secretary of the Catholic Institute of International Relations – puts it, the great *sacramental* act of today.)

I think the way forward has to reckon with where people really are. This is not to say we ought to conduct Church services on-line or baptise babies via e-mail. But it does mean paying more attention to the relationship of Christ to community.

We have fixed on Jesus as saving individual, as cosmic hero, rather than on his relationship with Messianic or saving community. We have even been in danger of what Dorothee Soelle – the German political theologian – has called *Christolatry*, even *Christofascism* – *namely, a divine saviour figure which focuses attention away from the saving energies at work in community itself*. Instead, the real core meaning of Christ is as *hope-in-the heart-of-community* (a meaning powerfully conveyed in an Indian hunger veil, depicting the Christ of the untouchables).

Two contemporary writers show a way forward. Mercy Amba Oduyoye was for years responsible for the Women's Desk at the World Council, President of the Ecumenical Association of Third World theologians, and a guest Professor at Princeton in the United States. As someone rooted in African experience of community where western individualism is just not intelligible, she understands Christ as a communal reality:

> Jesus *plus* the crowd, men and women, make up the image of God's anointed, the messiah who brings well-being.[4]

The saving role of Christ is an enterprise for the whole community in her theology.

Furthermore, this was ever the case – even in New Testament times. Thus Rita Nakashima Brock, an Asian-American theologian, in her Christology work *Journeys by Heart: a Christology of Erotic Power*[5] shows how Jesus was nurtured and ministered to by the messianic community itself, women and men. Salvation, the attainment of personal and community well-being is only experienced by relationships of mutuality, intimacy, in a structural setting of justice, promoting and upholding the dignity of the most weak and vulnerable categories in society. She particularly emphasises the role of women in the messianic community, pointing out that it was the women who stood by Jesus in his hours of agony and death. The courage to resist, and to be compassionate – literally *compassion*, together in suffering – meant that the women were empowered to receive the reality of resurrection, risen life.

It is this Christic Risen life which is what I call an organic, dynamic reality of salvation: *Christic presence as the praxis of community;* Christic presence as the patterning of messianic community. How can we know this, then, in a way which does not fall into the old traps

---

[4] This is taken from her forthcoming book: Oduyoye, *Introducing African Women-centred Theology* (Sheffield Academic Press, 1999).

[5] New York, Crossroads, 1989.

described earlier, and which meets the challenges of this post-modern, supermarket, cyber-culture?

MESSIANIC COMMUNITIES – SKETCHING A NEW MAP TOWARDS THE MILLENNIUM

All through history we recognise the spell which the idea of saving community, messianic community, discipleship of Christ, has cast in new and dynamic ways. The history of the Church has not been *totally* synonymous with disunity, violence and corruption. All of us cherish such memories as the springtime of the Franciscan movement, the inspiration of many religious congregations arising as response to a particular context, or specific need of society. Again and again we have had revolutionary Christian movements, from Thomas Müntzer to Gerrard Winstanley,[6] to the global movements of liberation Christians of today, as well as the Women Church movement and more recently, the *We are Church* movement. We have had communities of contemplative presence as well as contemporary efforts to embody contemplation, silence and action, with care for creation – like the Taizé and Iona communities. What I attempt here is to try to sketch what qualities make a community messianic and salvific in our approaching-the-millennium context.

First, every community must have identity, must be recognisable as a group. This must be true even if the grouping is very loose – and some communities deliberately have very fluid boundaries in order to be accessible and inclusive. (The question of boundary is crucial.) For example, many people wear a chain with a peace bird symbol. This is recognisable as a peace symbol fairly universally, as well as being a symbol of the Holy Spirit in Christianity, and in the project in India, *Wells for India,*[7] the Peace bird is the Gandhian symbol of inspiration. I

---

[6] For Müntzer and Winstanley see Andrew Bradstock, *Faith in the Revolution* (London, SPCK, 1997).

[7] Wells for India was co-founded by my husband Nicholas Grey, myself and Dr. Ramsahai Purohit, a Gandhian Peace and Inter-faith worker, to work for the integrated social development of poor communities in the desert of Rajasthan.

also believe that in a context of war, to wear a peace symbol conveys some kind of message in the public arena. And this is what I am looking for – symbols of saving community in our world of multinationals and supermarkets.

More crucial for identity is the question of owning a common history and culture. What do we share which moulds and kneads us together in a multi-cultural, multi-faith society? The temptation to fall into a patriotism and nationalism, into neo-imperialisms, intolerant of minority communities is something which authentic Christianity must resist. The way forward is to identify with those dimensions of Christian tradition which nurture the praxis of Christic living, which embody *communal* well-being – not only that of the privileged few.

So the question of *dream* and *vision* become central. How close is our community vision to the vision and project of Jesus, namely the reign of the Kingdom or the *kin-dom* of God?[8] The word *kin-dom* has become important in Christian feminist theology as embodying the family or web of just relations wherein we are all sisters and brothers in the beloved community.

But let not this be a dream solely for *here-after*. It is the embodying of the dream in the practical circumstances of here-and-now which identifies this as salvific. The three most important features I want to identify in the embodying of this dream are *memory, embodied grace* and *hope*.

Memory, or *dangerously re-membering,* generates new energy. It is has become an empowering resource for liberation for poor communities struggling for liberation. To be mindful – or in many cases to recover the memories which have been blotted out by the dominating powers – is a vital part of the salvific process. Jean-Baptist Metz, Elizabeth Fiorenza, Walter Benjamin, Sharon Welch – all writers on 'dangerous memory' – stress that memories are not only that of suffering, but of the once-experienced pride of identity, of culture, values and tradition.[9] I think of the current recovery of the culture of Celtic people – the love of art, poetry and music which is re-surfacing

---

[8]   See Ada-Maria Isasi-Diaz, *En La Lucha: A Hispanic Women's Liberation Theology* (Minneapolis, Fortress, 1993).

as we develop an aesthetic dimension of faith as counterbalance to an over-rationalised tradition. In India, the culture of the tribal people, indigenous to the land before the Aryans arrived, struggles for recognition in a dominant culture where tribal people are excluded from the caste-system. To re-member a Christ who reached out beyond the taboos of the day makes Christic presence empowering. For women today, the dangerous memory of the leadership, authority of women in the New Testament times – as well as in many different periods of Church history – is a source of empowerment today as we work towards a just community of women and men in the churches.

Then there is the embodying or earthing of grace, which names the concrete ways in which Christic presence works towards well-being, the common good. We name the graced efforts of ecological communities, literally redeeming the earth. (Think, for example, of Agenda 21, of the efforts of *Christian Ecology Link*, of *Christian Lifestyle* groups and so on.) I see salvation embodied here in the words of Rosemary Ruether as 'reconversion to the earth'.[10] Dorothee Soelle envisions the restored community in terms of the book of Genesis, where 'nature, animals and women partake of the joy, the fullness of the life of the garden'.[11] Many of these Christian ecological groups have fluid boundaries and have the humility to learn from groups outside Christianity which are blazing a torch in this direction. If we are to be a messianic community in the supermarket, this fluidity is essential. I see chaplaincies in University, College, prisons, hospitals and hospices, peace groups and factories, all working in this way.

The most impressive way in which structural grace is being embodied is the way the Jubilee coalition for the millennium is bringing all this together. Working across the denominations, and with all people of good-will, this coalition brings the prophetic agenda

[9] On the theme of dangerous memory, see M. Grey, 'The subversive memory of the poor', in *New Blackfriars*, November 1994.

[10] Ruether, cited in Keller, 'Talk about the Weather'.

[11] D. Soelle, *To Work and To Love: A Theology of Creation*, (Philadelphia, Fortress, 1984), 80– 1, 150.

of Jubilee – to set free the slaves and bonded labourers, cancel the debts and give back the land to whom it belongs – right into the heart of the millennium agenda and into the heart of the politics of the market-place.

But, most crucially of all is the way embedded grace is literally *grace-in-the body*. The *enfleshing of Christ* is the anointing and healing of the violated flesh of the weak and the vulnerable. It is the honouring of the bodies of battered women, abused children, and the discarded categories of people – like the mentally ill, the Alzheimer's sufferers – as society careers onward, glorifying the temporarily-abled, young and beautiful. Here we are far away from the idea of the saviour as *deus ex machina*. Embodied grace, the sacred healing of God, works through graced action between people, relational grace, the fragile reaching out, touching and being touched, the deep listening to the unheard and suppressed voices.

Hope, hope beyond hope, outrageous, beyond reason, persistent and unsuppressible is what sustains these movements of embodied grace. Mercy Amba Oduyoye refers to the hope which sustains African women as 'wearing hope like a skin'.[12] This hope is both wildly eschatological – that ultimately God's dream for the world, the *kin-dom of right relations* – will come to be; and at the same time, concrete and simple – and giving rise to celebration. Every small victory over darkness and injustice is embodied grace and cause for celebration. Water that flows again in the desert of Rajasthan; saplings beginning to sprout leaves; Fair Trade products on the shelves of the supermarkets and a rejection of products where there is no minimum wage guaranteed; local produce starting to be consumed in season instead of luxury products out of season; disabled people given their rightful dignity ... 'With joy you will draw water from the wells of salvation ...'.

---

[12] See Oduyoye, *op. cit.*, forthcoming.

Mary Grey

EPILOGUE: THE HOSPITALITY OF GOD

What draws together many of these dimensions is the *hospitality* and generosity of God. As we have seen, the root meaning of salvation is the *common well-being* the flourishing or blossoming of creation, summed up by the WCC process – justice, peace and integrity of creation. I use this notion – which has already been used by Letty Russell in her book *Church in the Round*[13] – the round table symbolising our Eucharistic hospitality to each other – because it is making ourselves and all we possess vulnerable to the other. *Our basic orientation reaches out towards being gifted-by and gifting the other.* In its most fundamental expression it means being hospitable to our own bodies – seeing in our own bodies and those of others, ageing and clumsy they may be, the image of the divine. It means making our dwelling places, our hearths and homes, our work-places and our streets, places of hospitality and welcome: eucharistic in their table-sharing and life-style. And finally, it means receiving embodied grace in the hospitality of earth, water, air and light, in the communities of soil and all living things. This is salvation – because it is *reconversion to God's hospitality,* away from the abuses of hospitality, in unjust immigration and deportation practices, for example, with a prison system based on punishment, taking revenge and no forgiveness; away from the abuse of the word *hospitality* in the case of sex tourism, prostitution and 'hospitality women'.

Most profound of all, *hospitality* points towards the boundless generosity of God, whose being is both shrouded in mystery, yet revealed as being-in-community. It is this Divine being-in-community whose intimations reveal themselves as embodied in a love which knows no boundaries, inclusive of the sparrows and the lilies of the fields, ceaselessly poured out until all beings, created and uncreated are touched by this life-giving and restoring grace.

[13] Letty Russell, *Church in the Round,* (Westminster, John Knox, 1993).

Salvation and the Self

David F. Ford

IN LYNNE BROUGHTON'S book, *Interpreting Lincoln Cathedral: the Medieval Imagery*[1], we are led through Lincoln Cathedral with an extraordinarily rich combination of architectural, artistic, historical and theological sensitivity. The Cathedral itself is revealed as a theatre of God's drama, performed in stone, colour, glass, and the shaping of space for the worship of God through the great biblical stories, the sacraments, and the rhythm of the church year. At the end of a tour that has become a pilgrimage through the heartlands of Christian faith and tradition she has an Epilogue entitled: 'Out of Zion, the Perfection of Beauty, God hath shined'. The shining of the face of God, one of the great and rather neglected biblical figures of salvation, is suggested as a suitable leading theme for this lecture in this place.[2]

1. A JOURNEY OF INTENSIFICATION: THE SELF IN WORSHIP

In this lecture I want to invite you on what David Tracy calls a 'journey of intensification'. I will not apologise for all the roads not taken. My path through the vast country of self and salvation will begin where Lynne Broughton's book places us: in the sphere of worship. My focus will be on the self being transformed and flourishing in the theatre of the worship of God. There will be three main stages. First, I will ask in a preliminary way, through dialogue with two twentieth century philosophers, about a concept of self which might do justice to the self in full worship of God. Second, in the main central section, I will explore the formation of self through

[1]   Lincoln Cathedral Publications, Lincoln, 1996.

[2]   This lecture draws on David F. Ford, *Self and Salvation. Being Transformed* (Cambridge University Press, Cambridge, 1998).

23

two classic engagements, with the word of the Bible and the sacrament of Holy Communion or the Eucharist. Finally, I will reflect on Jesus Christ as worshipper and worshipped.

2. THE FACING SELF

The self is a prime locus for crisis and transformation in modernity. This is especially so in late modernity or post-modernity, or whatever one calls our own time at the end of a century of massive changes, traumas and disillusionments. Two philosphers that I find especially perceptive and profound on the self in our century are the Lithuanian Jewish thinker Emmanuel Levinas (who became a professor of philosophy in the Sorbonne) and the French Protestant Paul Ricoeur. They themselves were friends, and the discussion between them is explicit in Ricoeur's work. I will elide the necessary complex analysis of their thought and how they relate to each other[3] in order to sketch what I learn from dialogue with them about the worshipping self.

First, there is the identification of what is at stake in contemporary debates and conflicts. Ricoeur's suggestion is that we need to find some concept of self that responds to the challenges of two extremes. There is, on the one hand, the excessively centred, self-positing self, associated with Descartes' quest for certainty and Kant's quest for autonomy; on the other hand, there is the fragmented self, the scattered self, associated with Nietzsche's radical suspicion and dissolution of centred subjectivity. Ricoeur's alternative is suggested by the title of his book, *Oneself As Another*.[4] The self is in intrinsic relation to others, and there is no level of self where others are not significant. Among the most intimate others are our own bodies, other persons and the imperatives, voices and faces before which we are answerable, and which he sums up in a rich notion of 'conscience'.

At the heart of Ricoeur's subtle thinking through of this concept of self is his wrestling with the challenge of Levinas's conception of selfhood in which the other person determines our selfhood by calling

[3] This is the subject of the best part of four chapters in *Self and Salvation*.

[4] University of Chicago Press, Chicago and London, 1992.

us to radical responsibility. One Levinas expression for this is 'the appeal in the face of the other', and 'the face' is one of his most fruitful philosophical ideas. He and Ricoeur together lead us to conceive of what one might call 'the facing self'. This self has all the marks of distinctive identity and life signified by the particularity of each face, but at the same time is itself through relating to others, especially in recognition and responsibility.

Worship can be seen as an intensification of the facing self. As we worship we are above all faced by God and face God. The truth of facing God is mediated in many ways, especially through the testimony of scripture and of other worshippers through history and around the world today. In facing a God who faces all humanity and all creation we too are invited to live within that universal horizon. And in Christian worship the nature and quality of that facing is embodied especially in one particular face, that of Jesus Christ. On this understanding,

> Christianity is characterised by the simplicity and complexity of facing: being faced by God, embodied in the face of Christ; turning to face Jesus Christ in faith; being members of a community of the face; seeing the face of God reflected in creation and especially in each human face, with all the faces in our heart related to the presence of the face of Christ; having an ethic of gentleness (*praütes*) towards each face; disclaiming any over-view of others and being content with massive agnosticism about how God is dealing with them; and having a vision of transformation before the face of Christ 'from glory to glory' that is cosmic in scope, with endless surprises for both Christians and others.[5]

In line with all this, salvation for the self might be seen as a comprehensive flourishing marked by full mutual hospitality in relation to God and other people, and full worship in response to the shining of the face of God (as evoked by Lynne Broughton's Epilogue). The rest of my lecture will explore aspects of this conception.

[5] Ford, *Self and Salvation*, pp. 24ff.

3. THE FORMATION OF THE WORSHIPPING SELF: WORD AND SACRAMENT

How is the worshipping self formed? The classic Christian answer is: through word and sacrament. That seems to me profoundly true – so profound, indeed, that we can never fathom its riches and need continually to rethink it, open to the ways in which, as worshipping selves, our minds, as well as our hearts, imaginations and wills, need to be open to continual transformation in order to try (always in vain) to cope with the abundance of God's truth, beauty and love. Above all, both word and sacrament testify to the endlessly creative and responsive love of God for us. That love stretches our love and understanding ever wider as, in little ways, we allow our lives to be shaped in response to it.[6]

My concern in what follows is not for the amazing diversity of ways in which people initially enter into this dynamic of transformative love. In other words, I will not say anything about conversion in response to the Gospel and only a little about the initiating sacrament of baptism. Rather, I will try to sketch what is involved for a baptized self who is shaped by the word in the form of the Letter to the Ephesians and by the sacrament in the form of the Holy Communion or the Eucharist.

3.1. EPHESIANS: THE SINGING SELF

So let us turn to the Letter to the Ephesians, which I will read as a portrayal of the worshipping self in Christian community, while recognizing that this many-faceted letter can also be read appropriately in several other ways. I take Ephesians[7] as probably written in Asia Minor towards the end of the first century by a

---

[6] Cf David F. Ford, *The Shape of Living* (Fount, Harper Collins, London 1997).

[7] One of the most helpful works on the theology of Ephesians against the background of recent scholarship is Andrew Lincoln's treatment in Andrew T. Lincoln and A. J. M. Wedderburn, *The Theology of the Later Pauline Letters* (Cambridge University Press, Cambridge, 1993).

follower of Paul. Paul had been the catalyst in the first major transposition of Christian faith to the Hellenistic cities of Asia Minor and Greece. In that (syncretistic) urban culture the faith underwent various modifications, and as the Pauline communities, such as that of Ephesus, entered their second generation they encountered the usual problems of continuity, adaptation and issues in practical living. The letter appears to be creative interpretation of Christian faith and life for a reasonably well-established community which is in need of strong affirmation of its identity.

For my purposes it is an extraordinarily fascinating example of 'the word'. In itself it combines a range of genres: liturgical forms such as eulogy, intercession, doxology, and hymn; creedal and confessional formulae and phrases; proclamation, catechesis, and other teaching material; and interpretation of scripture and of the Pauline tradition. It also says a good deal *about* communication. Chapters 1–3 speak especially about praise and proclamation. Chapters 4–6 say a great deal about the gifts, virtues, habits, and distortions of communication in the ordinary life of a long-term community. But above all it embodies the quality of communication that it talks about and makes it clear that the primary locus of this transformative communication is worship.

Apart from its opening greeting, Chapter 1 is an extended address in praise of God, and the location of the worshippers is emphasised over and over again as being 'in Christ'. In Chapter 2 this location of selfhood 'in Christ' is explained further: the 'new person' (*kainos anthropos*) Jesus Christ has, by his death, broken down the dividing wall between Jews and Gentiles. This is a reference to the wall in the Temple beyond which Gentile worshippers could not go. The culmination of the chapter is an image of the church as 'a holy temple in the Lord ... a spiritual dwelling for God' (vv. 21f). The description of salvation in terms of worshipping selves in community could not be plainer.

This is followed by a performance of worship in the prayer of 3.14–21, which I regard as the most daring prayer in the Bible. It asks extravagantly for strength, the indwelling of Christ, power to comprehend the incomprehensible love of Christ, and to be filled with all the fulness of God. One might think that would be enough, but the climax seems to imply not: God can 'accomplish abundantly far more than all we can ask or imagine' (v. 21). We have here a soteriology of abundance represented in a rhetoric of overflow, surpassing itself as it tries to do justice to a God who is 'always greater'.

Yet the most practical lesson on the formation of the worshipping self is yet to come. Pivoting between teaching addressed to the whole community (much of it on the ethics of speech) and instruction addressed to specific groups (husbands, wives, children, parents, masters, slaves) is 5.18–20:

> And do not get drunk with wine, for that is debauchery; but be filled with the Spirit, addressing one another in psalms and hymns and spiritual songs, singing and making melody to the Lord with all your heart, always and for everything giving thanks in the name of our Lord Jesus Christ to God the Father, being subject to one another out of reverence for Christ.

According to that, a Spirit-filled life means singing selves. Psalms, hymns and spiritual songs are, as it were, sacraments of speech, effecting what they signify: the performance of a differentiated yet harmonised community. The differentiation is in the encouragement to address one another in song; the harmony is in the proto-Trinitarian dynamic of united address 'in the name of our Lord Jesus Christ to God the Father' and the mutual subjection to one another. Singing in thanks is to be a pervasive, constant practice 'always and for everything'. Think of what this means for the filling of our time. Rowan Williams talks about a musical event as 'a recovery of the morality of time'.[8] Here in Ephesians we have a soteriology of time, time's transformation through music in the heart, for others and for God. Even the grammar of the Greek in v. 20 leads us to carry this sense on into the instructions about marriage and other relationships. The implication is that being subject to one another can be interpreted

[8] 'Keeping Time. For the Three Choirs Festival' in the *Open to Judgement* (DLT, London 1994).

through what goes on in good singing. Any notion of domination is neutralised – as reinforced by the subjection being 'to one another'. We are to imagine singing husbands and wives, singing parents and children, singing masters and slaves, with this singing 'in Christ' embracing them in a practice of self which can open them to further transformation 'in the Spirit'.

It is significant that singing is an intrinsically physical practice. It uses breathing, vocal chords, tongues, lips and ears, and it takes up the whole body into rhythms and movements. The body both gives energy to singing and is also energised by it. Singing can overflow into clapping, gesture and dancing. It can be of long-term significance, developing over time, improving with practice, and setting the tone of memories and associations.

> Bodily habits, rhythms and responses are formed by it. The injunction to be filled with the Spirit and sing is contrasted with 'Do not get drunk with wine' (f. 18). That in turn follows on from 5.16 where the exhortation is to 'make the most of the time, because the days are evil'. Drunkenness is a practice that incapacitates people for responsible use of time in line with 'the will of the Lord' (5.17). Singing psalms, hymns and spiritual songs, by contrast, enables a 'sober intoxication' which attunes the whole self – body, heart and mind – to a life attentive to others and to God. It is a practice of the self as physical as drinking – and as habit-forming. One of the main habits formed is that of alertness.[9] There is also the habit of obedience, a word closely connected in many languages with hearing. Singing is a model of free obedience, of following with others along a way that rings true. In this often the body leads the self, and we find ourselves absorbed in a meaning which only gradually unfolds and pervades other spheres.[10]

---

[9] Note the conclusion of 6.18: after 'Pray at all times in the Spirit' comes: 'To that end keep alert with all perseverance, making supplication for all the saints ...'

[10] Ford, *Self and Salvation*, p. 125.

So what emerges from Ephesians is an embodied self pervaded by the sung word. In song the self is intimately bound up with others, physically, emotionally, imaginatively and through rehearsing the truths of faith. And this self is identified not only with the contemporary community but with all those who have sung the psalms. The liturgical 'I' of the psalmist embraces each new worshipper in its capacious hospitality. The worshipper, thus linked into a vast community over time and space, yet also trusting in his or her own unique identity and affirmation by God (what the opening of Ephesians calls being chosen in love and destined for adoption as children, vv.4f), is neither a scattered, fragmented self nor a centred, self-positing and autonomous self. Instead, he or she is a 'self as another' intrinsically plural because in communion with fellow singers, yet always a distinctive face, freely responsible before the faces of others.

3.2. THE EUCHARISTIC SELF

I now turn to the Holy Communion or Eucharist. How is the self formed salvifically through regular eucharistic worship? This has historically been the main liturgical form in which that 'always and for everything giving thanks' enjoined in Ephesians has been realised – eucharist means 'thanks' – and clearly all that has been said about the singing self complements what might be said about eucharistic practice.

John MacIntyre, in his book *The Shape of Soteriology*,[11] asks why, when the early church produced developed definitions to do with Jesus Christ and the Trinity, it did not produce anything comparable about salvation. His answer is convincing: the Eucharist was its definition – not laid out in theology or creed, but performed in worship, perhaps every time the local church met together. Habituation to the Eucharist was the long-term ecology for the formation of Christian selves.

[11] T. & T. Clark, Edinburgh, 1992, p. 10.

That ecology had many niches, corresponding to the elements of the Eucharist. The Christian self in the habit of eucharistic worship was – and is – a self shaped through thanking, praising, repenting, interceding, petitioning, forgiving, promising, being immersed in the world of the Bible, following the church year, being taught, being warned, being judged, being encouraged, sharing the peace, sharing bread and wine, sharing money and goods, and being sent into the world in the power of the Holy Spirit. Most ideas of self are impoverished in comparison with what emerges from the rich practices and meanings of this celebration. It allows, in the words of the overall title of this series of lectures, for a 'scope of salvation' which embraces a dynamic interrelationship between God, other people and creation. This is realized through history and community, through giving and receiving hospitality, through multifaceted responsiveness in word and action, through learning and teaching, and through transformative alertness to the presence and activity of God in our world. Of course this ecology in particular ecclesial environments is never entirely healthy, and frequently suffers from evils ranging through the theological equivalents of holes in the ozone layer, atmospheric pollution, the dumping of toxic waste and too many chemical additives. But my focus is on salvation not on sin, and I want to ask how to characterise this eucharistic self at its best.

I will make one fundamental suggestion: that the Eucharist be understood as: *'The blessing of Jesus Christ'*. Blessing is

> a word whose biblical and traditional use enables us to maintain the priority of God without seeming to diminish humanity or creation. God blesses and is blessed, we bless and are blessed, creation blesses and is blessed, and a glorious ecology of blessing is the climactic vision of the Kingdom of God .... The Eucharist generates a habitus [Bourdieu] of blessing and offers a hospitality which incorporates people and the material world by blessing.[12]

The blessing of Jesus Christ is about receiving his blessing and about blessing him – the one whose very name, Jesus, means 'God

---

[12] Ford, *Self and Salvation*, p. 157.

saves'. The archetypal Christian sign of personal identity is baptism, when one identifies with Jesus's baptism, death and resurrection and with the baptism of every other Christian. There one is marked with the sign of the cross on the face, is baptized in the name of the Father, Son and Holy Spirit, and is blessed in the same name. But how can one ever learn to live with this God of superabundant blessing? The basic answer is: through habitual worship, and especially in the Eucharist. The Eucharist is an apprenticeship in coping with being blessed and with actively blessing God, other people and all creation. It is an active receptivity in which the primary signification is the passivity of being fed by bread and wine that have been blessed. A eucharistic self is, therefore, a baptized self in the routine of the community's 'family life', which sustains the human flourishing that is at the heart of salvation.

This is just a small beginning in exploring the self as formed through the Eucharist. I will mention even more briefly three further basic features of this self characterised by the blessing of Jesus Christ.

First, there is the new *placing* of self in the Eucharist. It is placed face to face with other people around (or before) a table (or altar), remembering the Last Supper at which Jesus faced and fed his disciples, and looking forward to a future feast in which he will be seen face to face.

> 'Maranatha! Come, Lord Jesus!', seems to have been the acclamation of the earliest Christians, and the rich tradition of 'the vision of God' has taken up that longing for an ultimate facing. The ultimate place is, therefore, in 'the light of the knowledge of the glory of God in the face of Christ' (2 Cor. 4: 6); and the transformation of self happens in that facing in faith: 'And we all, with unveiled face, beholding the glory of the Lord, are being changed into his likeness from one degree of glory to another; for this comes from the Lord who is the Spirit.' (2 Cor. 3: 18)[13]

So the Eucharist places the self before the face of Jesus Christ – remembered, present in the Spirit, and expected.

[13] *Ibid.*, p. 164.

Second, there is the new *timing* of the self through the Eucharist.

Baptism re-enacts the epoch-making event of Jesus Christ in its once and for all character. The Eucharist 'times' history with that event which is at the origin of our calendar; but it also relates to the timing of regular family meals, making bread, maturing wine, conversing and singing. History is punctuated with eucharists which can transfigure time through this interweaving of the ordinary and extraordinary [or epoch-making].[14]

So a self may be timed by the Eucharist, and this is realised existentially as the past is taken up through thanks and forgiveness, the present is pervaded by love and worship before the face of God, and the future is shaped through hope. We live in the convergence of many modes of timing – those of nature, of the members of our families, of our work, of financial markets and interest payments, of television schedules, of music, and so on. In the midst of all these, the Eucharist can be our *cantus firmus,* that basic shaping of time through which we can try to interrelate, judge and transform all the others. Above all, there is that great transformer of our time, death. The Eucharist imprints our lives with the memory of one death which relativises all other deaths. To be timed by the death and resurrection of Jesus Christ is to face the future with that blend of urgency and peace which was such a striking mark of the first Christians as they took on the risky and joyful responsibilities of living before the face of the crucified and risen Jesus Christ.

Third, there is the imperative invitation at the heart of that peaceful urgency. A eucharistic self is faced by the one who commands, 'Do this!'.

The participant in the Eucharist is therefore under an obedience which has its first (and, as Judas and Peter suggest, most testing) arena in relation to those around the table. There is a particularity of obedience to be constantly discerned in the contingencies of life. The central orientation for the formation of this obedient self is towards death. The imperative is to die to self, as enacted in

[14] *Ibid.,* p. 164.

baptism. The self that is formed [in the Eucharist] is awake to death and identified with a particular death. All repetition sets up expectation of the next repetition but also makes us sensitive to any changes. The repetition of the Eucharist sets up an expectation of death [recalling always its original dangerous moment on the eve of Jesus' death], and it allows participants to have an unrepressed sense of death; yet, at the same time, because death is now inseparable from the news of resurrection, it allows for daringly faithful improvisations of new life.[15]

Now, having considered the eucharistic self under the headings of blessing, placing, timing and commanding, let us remember that above all this is an other-oriented 'facing self'. The Eucharist

is not preoccupied with the cultivation of self but with being responsive to Jesus Christ and other people and coping with their responses in turn. The logic of this is not to become too concerned with the pattern of the Eucharist, significant though that is. What will help most [in acquiring the habitus?] in becoming a mature eucharistic self? At the practical level, the answer is obvious: practice. But thought and practice are inseparable, so a further question for a theological study such as this is: what sort of thought will help most? ... [T]he utterly essential matter for thought is indicated by the distinctive nature of the eucharistic habitus. Because it is oriented to Jesus Christ and to others the main energies of thought must be directed towards Jesus Christ and others.[16]

That simple principle dictates the final topic of this lecture: Jesus Christ, whom Dietrich Bonhoeffer described as 'the man for others'.

4. JESUS CHRIST, WORSHIPPER AND WORSHIPPED

Ephesians and the Eucharist clearly make the self of Jesus Christ an unavoidable topic in treating self and salvation. But clearly too it is not possible to explore the vast areas of theology this opens up,

---

[15] *Ibid.*, p. 165.

[16] *Ibid.*, p. 166.

especially the Trinity, christology and the relation between the person and work of Christ. What I want to do is to pursue my journey of intensification focussed on the worshipping self.

In relation to Jesus Christ, the central issue is clear, and so fundamental that it was the main doctrinal preoccupation of the formative centuries of Christianity: Jesus Christ is affirmed as the one self who is both worshipper and worshipped. What might this mean? I think it means a reconception of God, selfhood and worship simultaneously. To face this person, Jesus Christ, in faith is to find ourselves in a dynamic of worship in which the blessing of Jesus Christ is identified with the blessing of God, and Jesus Christ himself is affirmed as intrinsic to the reality of God. The most perceptive historical account of the pivotal events through which this came about is, in my opinion, given by Rowan Williams in his book *Arius*,[17] and of particular importance for my point is his 'Theological Postscript', which I regard as one of the most significant christological statements produced this century. Taking Rowan William's profound and innovative reaffirmation of the mainstream tradition for granted, how might we conceive the meaning and significance of Jesus Christ as worshipper and worshipped?

I will have to be content with a few basic suggestions, in the form of brief theses, each of which really requires at least a lecture to itself.

First, the life, teaching and ministry of Jesus are to be understood theologically as utterly centred on God and the Kingdom of God. Everything is referred to God and understood in relation to God and God's will for the flourishing of all creation.

Second, the testimony to Jesus is to the inseparability of his message from his person and fate. This is especially so at the climax of the story as he goes to Jerusalem and celebrates the Last Supper: 'This is my body', 'This is my blood'.

Third, as the Letter to the Hebrews was to develop most fully in the New Testament, the death of Jesus can be seen as an act of full worship. The basic form of offering in Israel's worship was sacrifice. The death of Jesus is his offering of all he embraces and all he is to his

[17] DLT, London, 1987.

David F. Ford

Father in trust and is appropriately conceived in sacrificial terms. In all four Gospels the death of Jesus is identified as worship by describing Jesus praying (or crying out) in the words of psalms. The most discussed is from Psalm 22 in Mark's and Matthew's accounts of Jesus on the cross:

> My God, my God, why has thou forsaken me?
> (Mk. 15: 34; Mt. 27: 46)

It is striking how this is answered within the psalm itself:

> ... he has not hid his face from him,
> but has heard, when he cried to him. (v. 24)

How are we to read that? I suggest that, on the one hand, this context should not be used to soften the dereliction of Jesus; but, on the other hand, it offers a way of understanding the resurrection as the salvific 'not hiding' of God's face which takes the form of the appearance of the crucified Jesus.[18]

[18] The other crucifixion psalms are also relevant to this. In Luke Jesus quotes Psalm 31 to his Father: 'Into your hand I commit my spirit. (v. 5). The context of this in the psalm is trust in God as saviour in extreme affliction and rejection of the worship of idols. Again the theme of salvation and the face of God appears:

> Let your face shine on your servant;
> save me in your unfailing love. (v. 16)
> You will hid me under the cover of your presence (*panim*)
> from those who conspire together ... (v. .20)
> In sudden alarm I said,
> 'I am shut out from your sight.'
> But you heard my plea
> when I called to you for help. (v.22)

In John 19: 28– 29 Jesus's cry 'I thirst' and the sponge of vinegar echo Psalm 69: 21, and that context includes the same theme:

> Do not hide your face from me, your servant;
> answer me without delay, for I am in dire straits. (v. 17)

It therefore makes sense to interpret the crucifixion of Jesus in terms of salvation and the facing of God.

This brings me to my fourth point, that the critical issue can be seen, in terms of the language of this lecture, as the relation between the dead face of Jesus on the cross and the face of the resurrected Jesus. Jesus's death can be seen as 'the utter differentiation of the worshipping human being from God. It is a complete self-offering which simply awaits God's response and is utterly dependent on it – which is how it could generate the classic Pauline, Augustinian and Lutheran doctrine of justification by faith. That response is the resurrection.'[19] The resurrection of the crucified Jesus is the God-sized event which allows us to reconceive simultaneously God, humanity and worship. Its 'logic' (most perceptively elucidated by Hans Frei in his major work *The Identity of Jesus Christ*)[20] is: God acts, Jesus appears, and the disciples are salvifically transformed. The reconception of God is in terms of the Trinity. The reconception of humanity is, as Rowan Williams makes clear,[21] seen in the true humanity of Jesus Christ as new humanity (the new Adam). The reconception of worship is the presupposition of both those developments. What about that worship?

Jesus Christ was intrinsic to Christian worship – was, in fact, as Ephesians makes clear, its theatre. I would suggest that John's Gospel is right in the implication of its resurrection accounts (which are epistemologically so subtle), when it has Thomas say to the risen Jesus: 'My Lord and my God!' This is borne out by forms of address to Jesus, by fragments of hymns, and above all by the new pattern of Christian worship in the Eucharist. It took hundreds of years to refine the conceptuality, but the language was there before its 'grammar' was articulated. In terms of some of the most primitive imagery, worship was directed towards God as the Father who was utterly in union with the one sitting at his right hand. To be before the face of God was to be before the face of the risen Jesus Christ.

[19] Ford, *Self and Salvation*, p. 213.

[20] Fortress Press, Philadelphia, 1975.

[21] *Op. cit.*

The transformation of worship is thorough. To have one person as worshipper and worshipped, rules out a conception of worship in which a subject, the worshipper, is directed towards a God conceived as a separate, undifferentiated object. Getting rid of that is a major step away from idolatry. Instead, God is free to take an initiative in order to lead us into worship from our side. Jesus is God in a way which tells us how to worship God. He embodies the facing of God and the facing of humanity. So there is facing, otherness, within God. There is even worship within God, a dynamic of love and glorification. The dead face is taken up as the pivotal moment of worship and glory – 'the lamb on the throne', 'the lamb slain since before the foundation of the world' (Rev. 13: 8). The self of Jesus, given for other in worship of God, is the reconstitution of facing and so is saviour and salvation. In Ricoeur's terms, he is a human self *as* (in Ricoeur's fullest ontological sense) the other who is God; he is also a human self as the other who is [identified with] each person he faces. Salvation for the self is therefore to be 'christomorphic' in its facing of him and 'being transformed from glory to glory'.

To worship in faith before this face is above all to be faced by him. Whatever refers us to this face – whether the faces of fellow human beings, or the imagination aroused by scripture and worship, or works of art, or [radical and] joyful responsibility [or Christ incognito in the poor and marginalized,] or 'the face of the earth' ... leads us to 'see' Jesus Christ only to find ourselves 'more radically looked at',[22] loved, delighted in and accountable. And even 'seeing' this face in faith is to find it a self-effacing face, referring us to the face of the Father and to the faces of [all] fellow human beings.[23]

So this is the scope of salvation as understood in the theatre of the worship of this God. It is about the flourishing of all humanity and creation before a self-effacing God.

[22] Jean-Luc Marion, *God Without Being*, p. 22.

[23] *Ibid.*, p. 214.

'Out of Zion, the Perfection of Beauty, God hath shined'. That light takes many forms, and I would argue that they are not nearly so competitive with each other as has often been held. We Christians are called to an apprenticeship in being blessed, in blessing, and in transformative self-effacement before Jesus Christ in whom the face of God in the Aaronic blessing is recognized:

> The Lord bless you and keep you:
> The Lord make his face to shine upon you,
> and be gracious to you:
> The Lord lift up his countenance upon you,
> and give you peace.
>
> (Numbers 6: 24– 26)

Salvation and Creation:
'All Things New'

Richard Bauckham and Trevor Hart

THE THEME OF THIS lecture is salvation in its widest extent, extending to the whole of God's creation. The argument runs through four sections, beginning and ending with the Christian understanding of salvation, but on the way interacting with two non-Christian views of salvation which have been or are influential in our society. In this way we shall be situating the Christian view within our contemporary context, relating it to the issues that concern our society, and also clarifying it in its resemblances and contrasts with alternative approaches.

1. THE SCOPE OF SALVATION IN CHRIST (Richard Bauckham)

In the penultimate chapter of the Bible, in the opening statement of the very last speech God makes in the whole of the Christian Scriptures, God says: 'Behold I am making all things new' (Rev. 21: 5). The prophet sees the old heavens and the old earth – the universe as it now is – passing away, and new heavens and a new earth, God's new creation of all things, coming into being. It is not that God replaces the present world with another one. God makes the old new. God makes all things new. The God who here calls himself the Alpha and the Omega, the beginning and the end of creation (21: 6), the God who created all things in the beginning now brings all things redeemed and renewed into his eternal glory. This is how the story the Bible tells from Genesis to Revelation, the story we summarize in the Christian creeds, the story we live and take part in as Christians, the great story of all things that gives the world its Christian meaning, is to end: in the fulfilment of God's purposes for all things. 'Behold I am making all things new': this is the happy ending of all happy endings, the happy ending beyond all the tragic endings, the happily ever after of all creation.

The language of making old things new is one of the ways the Bible speaks about salvation. Paul uses it of our own salvation as individual Christians: 'If anyone is in Christ – there is a new creation' (2 Cor. 5: 17). But his use of the language in that way is to remind us that our own salvation as individuals is part of something very much greater. When people come to faith and find themselves in Christ, there is the new creation of all things beginning to happen. Salvation does not, as it were, single us out from the rest of God's creation. God's purpose is to save us in our solidarity with the rest of God's creation. So in our experience of the salvation we find in Jesus Christ we are discovering our place in the whole world as it will be when all evil and suffering, transience and death are over and done with, and all things live in the life of God eternally.

We might call this universal salvation, except that term tends to be used for the view (not the traditional Christian view) that every human individual will necessarily be saved in the end. That is a different issue, which we are not discussing in the present context. What I have described might be better called holistic salvation. In other words, salvation encompasses every aspect of God's creation. Salvation is of whole human persons: body, soul and spirit. Salvation is of humans in our community with each other, not as isolated individuals. Salvation is of the whole of God's creation, not just of humans. We humans are saved in our inextricable solidarity with the rest of God's creation. God's renewal of all things is the redemption and fulfilment of human history and also the redemption and fulfilment of nature and the final reconciliation of the two. But although this has always been the orthodox faith of the Christian mainstream, Christians have often had difficulty believing it. Various intellectual and religious tendencies within the church and outside the church have constantly inclined people to restrict the scope of salvation. Gnosticism and Platonism sowed deep suspicion of the bodily and material aspects of creation. Salvation must be of human spirits, freed from their temporary embodiment. And because our bodies are what obviously connect us with the rest of creation, spiritual salvation from bodies, leaving aside our bodies, has usually meant spiritual salvation from nature too. The material world, all God's non-human creatures, all their beauty and wonder, are considered disposable, serving their purpose merely as a temporary hotel for human spirits on their way to their true home in a non-material heaven. We need to ask ourselves whether this non-orthodox but very influential view of the natural world as temporary and disposable by God has not encouraged us to treat it as already disposable by us.

In the church's struggle with Gnosticism in the early centuries, it was the wholeness of Christian salvation, including the resurrection of the body and the redemption of all things, which had to be affirmed and was strongly affirmed by the church of that period. We need to recover it again today, when it is still the case that alternative views of salvation fall short of this all-encompassing Christian hope of the renewal of all things. For, although salvation is largely a Christian term, there are powerful secular myths of salvation which have shaped our society in the modern period and still exercise influence. Without exception such secular myths offer salvation only of a considerably restricted scope. They aspire to replace the God who makes all things new, but prove incompetent to do so. And for this reason they also prove more destructive than salvific.

2. THE DECLINE OF PROGRESS (Richard Bauckham)

We live at a critical juncture in the history of western society. As the third millennium approaches, western society finds itself bereft of a story to live by, lacking a worldview which can give meaning and hope for the world and the future. From within the churches, most of us are probably most conscious of the rapid decline of religous belief. For example, the recently revised schedules for Radio 4 continue the marginalization of religion even for that most church-going of mass media audiences. But there is another kind of belief which has declined as steadily during this century as religion: the belief in progress. By that I mean the myth which reads human history as a progressive advance from barbarism to utopia. This is the myth by which the whole modern age, from the Enlightenment of the eighteenth century onwards, has lived. It is the myth which has fired all the great projects of modern western humanity: education, science, technology, imperialism, democracy, unlimited economic growth. All the continuous and constantly increasing changes of modern western society over two hundred years have been sustained by this myth. We have lived with them and lived through them, optimistically, enthusiastically, taking the rough with the smooth because we believed them to be the route to utopia. This myth I think we can pronounce dead, though its influence persists. I am sure its decline could also be charted in the contents of Radio 4 over the decades, less easily because it has never been confined to a thought for the day or a daily service, but was once the ideology expressed in most serious programmes, though gradually less and less so.

Modern secular society – though for this reason postmodern society is a better description – now lives not only after the death of God, but also after the death of the myth of progress. The ghost of progress still haunts us, especially in the corridors of power, but it is the ghost of a dead ideology. It lingers in people's minds – not least Christian people's minds – more as an unexamined assumption than as a working faith. I shall be surprised if even the year 2000 gives it a new lease of life, though perhaps that is possible. We shall ask in a moment why it has declined so much in our century.

First we should consider how, as a myth of salvation, it compares and contrasts with the Christian one. I will make two points.

(1) Progress is the myth of immanent salvation. This means that salvation emerges from the process of human history. It is history itself which contains the dynamic and the resources for a steady advance towards utopia, and the goal of the process, whether it is envisaged as a final utopian condition, a posthistorical age, or as simply endless improvement without limit, is a product of the process itself. By contrast, the traditional Christian view placed its hope for salvation in the transcendent God, who is beyond the world and its

history as well as within it, the God from whose transcendent possibilities the world was first created and whose power to renew his creation far transcends the immanent capacities of creation itself. In the Christian view the new creation in which all things will find their goal will not be the product of human history, but the fresh creative act of the transcendent God, who, of course, fulfils the possibilities inherent in creation but also far surpasses them.

(2) If, for the myth of progress, human history is the sole *vehicle* of salvation, the principal *means* of salvation is the technological domination of nature. Progress means (not only but especially) humanity's progressive liberation of ourselves from nature and the progressive refashioning of nature into a world we have made to serve our ends. The whole scientific-technological project of the modern age has been a kind of new creation, a re-creating of the world by its godlike human masters. What happened in the development of the myth of progress was really that the Christian hope for all-encompassing salvation was reduced to human history, with its limited scope and capacities, while at the same time the historical process was invested with much of the transcendent expectations of the Christian hope. Human history was burdened with the impossible dream of achieving a new creation. Such a dream was always bound to founder fatally on the real limits of the present creation, which is all it has to work with.

Why has the myth of progress declined from its heyday in the nineteenth century to its slow death in the later twentieth century? The course of events in our century has simply refuted it. There are above all the horrors of twentieth-century history – 'the most bestial period in human history', as George Steiner calls it. The two World Wars, the Holocaust, Stalin's reign of terror, Vietnam, and the killing-fields of Cambodia, Bosnia and Rwanda are merely the better known, representative instances of the massively unprecedented scale of human violence in which literally hundreds of millions have died. These horrors do more than demonstrate the lack of progress. They make it impossible to view the evils and sufferings of history as justified by history's goal. If these horrors – children burned alive in

Auschwitz or buried alive in Cambodia – are the price of progress, then progress is not progress. What utopia could ever compensate for these?

But there is more. Not only has the technology on which progress depends been deeply implicated in these horrors – as well as even worse in prospect: nuclear weapons and ever more sophisticated biological weapons; not only has the myth of progress itself been the justification for some of the horrors, justifying the eggs broken for the sake of the utopian omelette to come: even many of the changes which seem most unequivocally beneficial for human life have come to threaten human life, not to mention the rest of life. Coming up against the ecological limits of life on this planet, for which the modern project with its godlike aspirations never sufficiently allowed, progress has turned against us. Yet its momentum – technological and economic – seems unstoppable. The myth of progress has worked its way so deeply into the warp and woof of our society – and more or less the whole world now – that whether we believe in it or not seems to make little difference to its now destructive course. It is the idol that once created holds its creators in thrall.

Did it have to be like this? In a very important sense, yes it did. There have been more and less benign versions of the myth of progress, more and less promethean versions. Perhaps the real benefits of the modern project could have been had with fewer of its calamities. But the disastrous error lay in the concept of a salvation immanent in human history. The critical question is: can human history be itself the source and vehicle of salvation? Can human history in and of itself overcome the experienced evils of life and fulfil the aspirations of humanity for qualitatively better life? A negative answer is required if we take on board the following three criticisms of the modern myth of progress, essentially criticisms made from postmodern and green (not necessarily Christian) perspectives:

(1) In practice, the myth of progress, despite its association with egalitarian and democratic ideologies, turns out to be elitist. It identifies progress with particular cultural projects – those of the modern west – and benefits only those in the vanguard of historical

progress so defined. The dead are forgotten. Those who suffered the evils of the past have paid the price for a possible utopia only their descendents can enjoy. Even those whose suffering now is beyond help must be left aside. The myth of progress takes a necessarily hardhearted view of the dead and the wretched of the earth, turning resolutely away from them lest its bright-eyed optimism be dimmed. If human history is the source and vehicle of salvation, this must be the case.

(2) Therefore the myth of progress has functioned as an ideology of domination. This is the postmodern critique, sometimes exaggerated but unquestionably true to a significant degree. The myth of progress has served to legitimate the exercise of power: imperial and communist regimes until recently, now primarily the west's economic domination over the third world, the power of the affluent over the poor, even the power of men over women. Since progress is identified with the values of some, the domination of these over others is justified. Progress is an ideology justifying history's victors, neglecting history's victims. If human history is the source and vehicle of salvation, this must be the case.

(3) Finally, the myth of progress has also meant the destructive domination of nature. Nature is subjugated and absorbed into history. Its only role is to be the raw material from which human history fashions its utopia. Again, if human history is the source of vehicle of salvation, this must be the case.

3.   THE NEW AGE ALTERNATIVE (Trevor Hart)

Human beings are resourceful creatures at the best of times; and at the worst; and we do not find it easy (perhaps even possible) to live for long without hope, or in the absence of something to look forward to. We need some sense of direction, of purpose, of meaning attaching to our existence. We want to know where we are headed. We crave what literary critic Frank Kermode has dubbed 'a sense of an ending' to our individual and our shared stories. The failure of the myth of progress to furnish a satisfying ending for us therefore threatens to cast us into a despairing meaninglessness, a literally hopeless situation in which our very humanity itself is at stake. The presence and reality of this threat should be all too apparent to anyone who pauses to consider the brooding sense of apathy, moral disorientation and even nihilism which characterizes so much postmodern culture, and which is busily shaping the desires and imaginations of the next generation. It is not surprising, then, that in the very same decades which have witnessed the final disillusionment with and unmasking of the myth's failure to deliver, we have also witnessed the emergence of an alternative contender, a champion to bear our hopes and deliver us from the titanic forces of chaos and historical entropy. I refer to that kaleidoscopic mixture of beliefs, rituals and fads which can be found gathered together on certain shelves in any branch of Waterstone's or Dillons, and which for convenience are usually referred to under the umbrella term New Age.

The term itself is suggestive, and points to one central underlying emphasis of the phenomenon: namely, that the bad old days in which we have been living for so long will not deliver salvation; some new way, some new stage of human understanding or way of being in the world needs to be embraced if we are to avert the ecological, military, social, physical and spiritual disasters which are the legacy of modernity's abortive attempt to 'play God' with the world. To this end the New Age offers a wide range of carefully marketed creeds, techniques and alternative therapies all designed to facilitate personal, spiritual, social and finally cosmic transformation in a world which otherwise seems doomed to hell. At its more serious and reflective (as opposed to its commercial and faddish) end New Age *begins* with the failure of history. The misplaced hopes of several centuries in western society have created the problem from which, New Age gurus tell us, we need to be delivered, and quickly. The new world (one might even say new humanity) which New Agers envisage in this sense lies 'beyond history'. It will only be realized, that is to say, by a radical and far reaching change of direction, leaving behind the assumptions and practices which have dominated the western mind for so long, and embracing a quite different way of thinking and behaving. Unlike modernity's myth, New Age is not optimistic about the essential human condition (not in the short term at least): it sees us, we might say, as essentially fallen and in need of radical redemption.

This, though, is only one side of the story. For in its wider perspective New Age is very optimistic, at least about the capacities of humankind to attain to redemption. In the wider New Age scheme of things, the period of moral, spiritual and ecological crisis in which we are currently living represents the final death throes of one stage in the evolution of human spiritual and physical existence, the conflict out of which a higher stage will duly emerge. In this sense the looked for New Age (which for reasons we don't have time to chart has been associated calendrically with the approaching millennium) will be precisely the summit, the *telos*, the true end of the human story. Some New Agers seem to view the arrival of this utopia as inevitable, something which is bound to happen. Others stress the need for people to seize what may otherwise prove to be a fleeting opportunity for salvation. The appearance of *homo spiritualis*, the attainment of the evolutionary 'Omega Point' (a phrase coined by and made popular in the writings of the Jesuit palaeontologist Pierre Teilhard de Chardin), the reversal of the momentum of history in the direction of a new world, all these may prove to have been contingent on the choices and lifestyles which we make in the closing decades of the twentieth century. It's quite some responsibility.

One of the most distinctive features of New Age is its essential monism: that is to say, it stresses repeatedly that all reality is ultimately *one*. We are one *both* with the physical cosmos and its processes (nature) *and* with the spiritual world which permeates it. We are not aloof from our physical environment, but bound up with it in a relationship of interdependence. Similarly, there is no 'God' up there apart from us; we are all part of 'God', part, that is to say, of the vast spiritual internet of energy which is the mesh around which the cosmos as a whole is woven. Grasping this emphasis helps us to understand two particular features of New Age.

First, its ecological dimension. Nature is not *something else* which is there simply as a stage for us to play out the human story upon, or as a warehouse of raw materials for us to plunder. Nature is *bigger* than us, but it is the big reality of which we are part and which gives us life. It is our womb, our Mother. The rape of nature is thus the most unnatural of relations and we should not be surprised if it leads to dark consequences. If, however, instead of struggling against and plundering nature through technology, we tune in to its 'natural' patterns and forces, if we learn to cooperate with nature, to live within its flow, then nature itself will furnish the route to our salvation. It will move to its natural end, and bear us with it.

Second, because we are part of nature, because we have natural access to the spiritual superstructure of reality (the 'control panel' of cosmic change as one New Age writer describes it), we have both the capacity and the responsibility to save the world and with it ourselves. Nature, in other words, cannot save us without our cooperation, our striving. Things *can* be different. But it's up to you to make them different. That is essentially the message which the New Age proclaims. Through a sufficient number of people embracing personal and spiritual transformation, submitted to the right disciplines and practices, embracing the right vision of reality and living in accordance with that vision, we have the power to transform society and ultimately to heal nature. It will be a radical and costly repentance; but for New Agers the salvation to which it will lead is available in no other way. To cite Marilyn Ferguson, the doyenne of serious New Age reflection, 'The myth of the saviour "out there" is being replaced with the myth of the hero "in here". Its ultimate expression is the discovery of the divinity within us'.[1] It is up to us to grasp our spiritual destiny and thereby to transform reality. Even at this late stage in the human story we, the central characters, can seize control of the plot and fashion a happy rather than a tragic ending.

In 1980 when Ferguson wrote her now classic mission-statement-cum-Bible of the New Age, *The Aquarian Conspiracy*,[2] she clearly

---

[1] Cited in Chandler, *Understanding the New Age* (Word Books, Dallas, 1988), p. 30.

[2] Paladin, London, 1982.

believed that she was witnessing unmistakable evidence that just such a sea change, just such a revolution was about to happen. The spiritually aware but spiritually starving masses were beginning to rediscover their essential divinity in hordes, and would soon overthrow in a peaceful revolution the failed world-view associated with the myth of progress. Minds were being expanded, consciousnesses transformed, and lives attuned with nature all over the western world. Almost twenty years on, though, it would seem that the note of optimism sounded in Ferguson's book was at best premature and more likely wholly misplaced. The critical mass of born again heirs to the Age of Aquarius has not been reached. Tribalistic nationalism, wars and violence, political and economic inequities have not abated, let alone been abolished. If anything it seems that they have received a considerable new lease of life. The much heralded 'new world order' and other political movements laying claim to the superficially attractive epithet 'new' seem, once an admitted shift in rhetoric is discounted, to offer much the same old diet of limited options, and manifest an incapacity or lack of will really to change anything in any very significant way. In addition to this the New Age phenomenon itself has hardly made any serious strides forward in terms of offering a credible alternative shared human agenda, and parts of it have developed in ways which accord ill with Ferguson's vision. It is ironic, given Ferguson's expressed disdain for certain economic models and their negative impact on society, that the New Age has itself spawned a veritable industry of vigorously marketed and commercially lucrative products from books and CDs, crystals and amulets, to expensive management training courses offered to industry, the latter, of course, designed precisely to enhance productivity and personal profit. It is difficult to escape the impression that the New Age phenomenon was overtaken by the political and economic climate of the eighties and has been very much conformed to this world, furnishing yuppy and post-yuppy culture with a hypermarket of options in spirituality without commitment, stimuli to cosmic speculation (from Nostradamus to the X–files), and techniques for personal advancement.

In truth the word 'new' itself, here and elsewhere, so often seems only to designate the same old reality with a careful 'spin' put on it. Or, to use a more post-modern way of describing things, it alludes to a different way of configuring or construing reality. The New Age alternative to the myth of progress is a construal of nature as essentially fitted to deliver us into utopia: all we must do is to seize the moment and cooperate for all we are worth. The problem for humanity at the end of the twentieth century, though, appears to be that no matter how we choose to construe it, reality itself keeps on rudely interrupting our illusions, forcing us to reckon with the uncomfortable likelihood that neither history nor nature bears within itself sufficient resources for its or our salvation. However laudable and good in themselves many of the principles gathered under the rubric of New Age may be (and however much we may prefer them to those of the myth of progress), rearranging the deckchairs on the Titanic and calling it a new way forward will not actually melt the iceberg of finitude which threatens to wreck our dreams. For imagination constrained by the limited possibilities of immanence it seems that there is little genuine hope to be had.

4. ALL THINGS MADE NEW – CHRISTIAN SALVATION (Trevor Hart)

Can it be that the loss and pain of this world, the waste and frustration which besets so many human and non-human lives, the unfulfilled promise, thwarted aspirations, missed opportunities and dashed hopes, will all finally be sealed as we, together with the rest of nature, are swallowed up by the black hole of nothingness? The Christian hope insists that it is not so, and in doing so resonates with that protest against ultimate meaninglessness in which every human cry of pain participates.

Wilfred Owen's poem 'Futility' gives voice to the innate human incredulity in the face of the apparent finality of death:

> Move him into the sun –
> Gently its touch awoke him once,
> At home, whispering of fields unsown.

....

> Think how it wakes the seeds –
> Woke, once, the clays of a cold star.
> Are limbs, so dear-achieved, are sides,
> Full-nerved – still warm – too hard to stir?
> Was it for this the clay grew tall? ....

In the libretto of Britten's *War Requiem* these words (and others like them) are juxtaposed provocatively with extracts from the Christian liturgy. The poet's tortured closing inquiry, 'O what made fatuous sunbeams toil/To break earth's sleep at all?', is met with the ancient invocation 'all pitying Lord Jesus, grant them rest', and set within the wider context of prayers for eternal light and the transition from death to life promised to Abraham and his seed.

The tension which this juxtaposition creates directs us to the distinctiveness of Christian hope, wherein its capacity to furnish imaginative resources for hope actually lies. The point is that the tragic dimensions of human life cannot and will not be resolved within the boundaries of either history or nature. Neither the most advanced technologies nor the sun's warming and otherwise life-giving rays can address the futile loss to which the poet bears witness. If this is true at the level of individual finitude then it is all the more so in relation to the meaningfulness and fulfilment of the human story as a whole. If this story is to have a comic rather than a tragic ending, we might say, then, as is the case in so many literary comedies, the ending will be unexpected, improbable in terms of the direction of the story as a whole. It will be a *divina commedia*, a divine comedy in which it is only by the contrivance of the God of the resurrection, the God who is able to bring life out of death, being out of non-being, that all is resolved well, and everything finally works together for good. Nothing within the possibilities and potentialities of nature or human history considered in themselves could account for a more than tragic end to the human story. But within the logic of Christian faith it is not the possibilities of the finite that we are called to invest our trust in, but the God with and for whom all things are possible. How the world will end is something which in the strictest sense lies currently beyond our imagining; but faith is offered images in terms of which to imagine the unimaginable: A world with no more war, no more suffering, no more death, no more loss. A world in which all the unfulfilled potential of history will somehow be taken up into fulfilment, all losses made good, all injustices set to rights. A world in which the hegemony of death will be broken open and swallowed up in the establishment of life in all its fullness.

Thus it is precisely by an imaginative appeal of hope *beyond* the limits of the historical and natural orders that Christian faith is sustained. All things will not *become* new through some natural process or human programme of works, but will be *made* new: made new, that is to say, by the same creator God who made them in the first place, the Father made known to us in his Son, Jesus Christ. Thus this is a *genuine* newness, a creative newness which wholly transcends the state of the here and now without yet collapsing into a novelty in which this present creation is abandoned or set aside in the preference for some other.

Is the object of Christian hope, then, firmly fixed in the future? As with all good theological questions, the answer to this one has to be Yes, and No! Yes insofar as the new creation itself, the new creative act of God which will wholly transform the cosmos, lies in the future. But no insofar as that same future is already being anticipated in this world in scattered acts of recreative anticipation, as the same Spirit which raised Jesus from death calls into being life, health, faith and hope where there is otherwise no capacity for these and no accounting for them. Such anticipations are to be found *in* this world, but they do not, properly speaking, *belong* to it. They belong to God's promised future, of which they are heralds, and towards which they direct our hopeful gaze. Thus we are not, as Christians, called to sit back and wait for God to make all things new. Christian faith is very much a matter of being ' in the meanwhile'. And in the meanwhile we are called to live in the light of this same hope, to recognize and to be involved with God's Spirit in all that he is doing to create genuine anticipations of the new in the midst of the old. Thus hope is a dynamic affair; it involves us in a struggle with the principalities and powers of this word, a struggle in which we are liberated from fear and guilt by the knowledge that we cannot win, in and of ourselves at least; but a struggle in which we are encouraged by the equally firm conviction that with the God and Father of Jesus Christ all things are possible, and he has promised to make all things new.